Selected Duets

for VIOLIN

Compiled, Arranged, and Edited by

HARVEY S. WHISTLER and HERMAN A. HUMMEL

Published In Two Volumes:

● VOLUME I (First Position – Medium) VOLUME II (First Position – Advanced)

CONTENTS OF VOLUME I

		Page
AIR DE BALLET	Blumenthal	7
ALBUMLEAF	Hohmann	34
ALLEGRO FROM THE FIFTH DUO	Pleyel	32
ALLEGRO FROM THE FOURTH DUO	Pleyel	20
ANDANTE-CAPRICE	De Beriot	6
AU PRINTEMPS	Viotti	35
BALLET-MÉLODIE	Mazas	18
BURLESKE	Tours	31
CARNAVAL	Alard	12
CHANSON BOHÉMIENNE	Kalliwoda	16
DANSE ÉCOSSAIS	Wichtl	25
DIVERTISSEMENT	Kalliwoda	14
DUO DE CONCERT	Wohlfahrt	36
EDELWEISS	Eichberg	8
ELFENTANZ	Eichberg	39
EPISODE	Eichberg	13
FEST-MARSCH	Weiss	40
KONTRATANZ	Kalliwoda	29
LA BANDOLINE	Kalliwoda	22
LA FARFALLETTA	Campagnoli	19
MARCHE CÉLÈBRE	De Beriot	2
MARCHE-PROCESSIONNEL	Dancla	9
MARSCH-PRÄLUDIUM	Gebauer	26
MENUET AND TRIO FROM THE FOURTH DUO	Pleyel	23
MENUET FROM THE FIRST DUO	Pleyel	4
MORCEAU DE CONCERT	Wichtl	17
MORCEAU DE SALON	Ries	30
NOVELLETTE	Eichberg	28
PANTOMIME	Kalliwoda	24
RIGAUDON	Kalliwoda	3
SILHOUETTE	Jansa	38
SOLITUDE	Dancla	10
VALSE-ETUDE	Dancla	11

7777 W. BLUEMOUND RD. P.O. BOX 13819 MILWAUKEE, WI 53213

Marche Célèbre

Rigaudon

KALLIWODA

Menuet from the First Duo

mp
mf
f
ff
rall.

Andante - Caprice

Air de Ballet

BLUMENTHAL

Edelweiss

EICHBERG

Marche - Processionnel

Solitude

DANCLA
Andantino e tranquillo
mf
mp
mf
mp
mf
mp
rit.
mf a tempo
mp
rit.
f a tempo
dim.

Valse-Etude

Elegante e leggiero

DANCLA

Carnaval

Tempo giusto
ALARD
mf-f

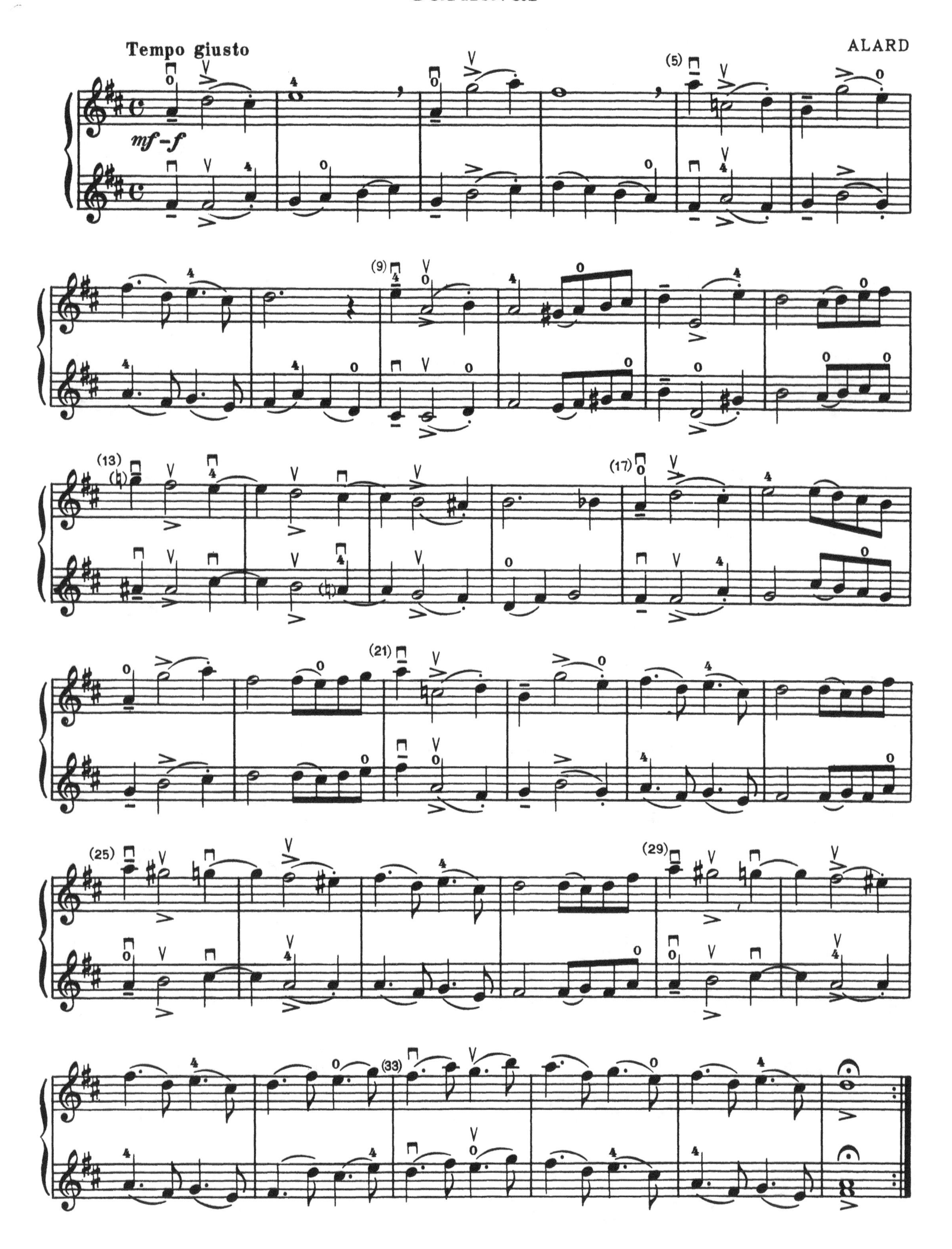

Episode

Commodo e tranquillo
EICHBERG
mp–mf
rit.

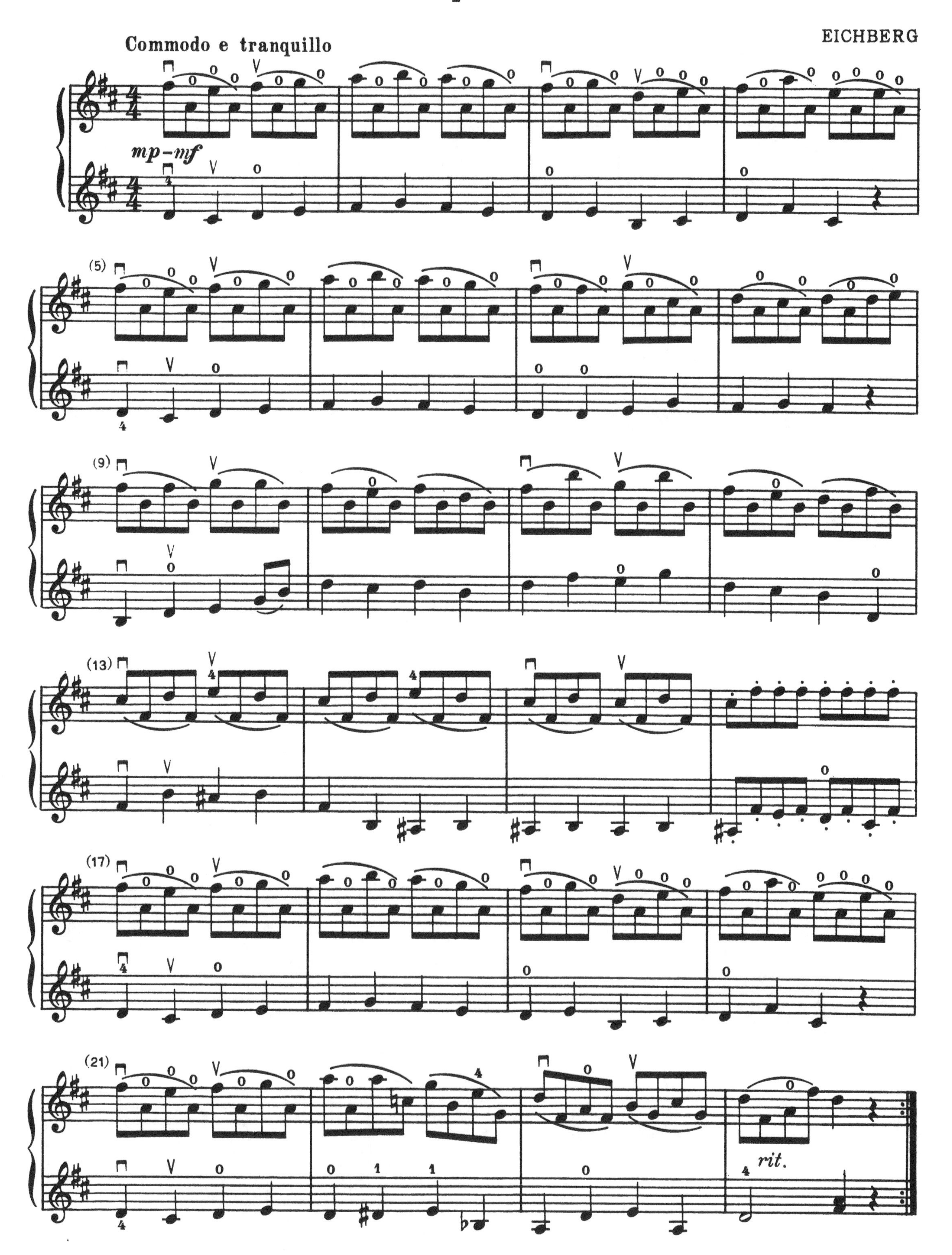

Divertissement

(38)
mf–f
(42)
(46)
(50)
(54)
(58)
(62)
(65)
(69)
cresc.
(73)
Fr.

Chanson Bohémienne

Morceau de Concert

Ballet-Mélodie

La Farfalletta

Allegro from the Fourth Duo

(49)
mp
(55)
mf
(60)
f
mf
(64)
(68)
mf
(72)
f
(77)
accel.
p
(80)
mf
(85)
sfz
sfz

La Bandoline

Menuet and Trio from the Fourth Duo

PLEYEL

Pantomime

Bene placito **KALLIWODA**

Danse Écossais
WICHTL
Allegro risoluto
mf–f
mf–f

Marsch-Präludium

GEBAUER

(40)
(44)
Fr.
(48)
(52)
(56)
(60)
(64)
(67)
(71)
ff

Novellette
Moderato molto
EICHBERG
f-ff
Fr.

Kontratanz

KALLIWODA

Morceau de Salon

Burleske

TOURS

Allegro from the Fifth Duo

(34)
Fr.
Fr.
Fr.
(38)
(41)
(45)
Fr.
(49)
(53)
(57)

Albumleaf

HOHMANN

Au Printemps

VIOTTI

Duo de Concert

WOHLFAHRT

(33)
(37)
(41)
mf
(45)
f
(49)
mf
(53)
f Fr.
(57)
(61)
(64)
allarg.

Silhouette

JANSA

Elfentanz

EICHBERG

Fest-Marsch

Allegro brillante
WEISS
f
(3)
(6)
f
(10)
mf
(14)
f
(18)
ff
(22)
f
(26)
ff
(28)